Dinosaurs That Ate Meat

by Leonie Bennett

Consultant: Mitch Cronick

BEARPORT
PUBLISHING COMPANY, INC.
New York, New York

Credits

Corbis: Page 13; Dinosaur artwork courtesy of ticktock Media Ltd.

Library of Congress Cataloging-in-Publication Data

Bennett, Leonie.
    Dinosaurs that ate meat / by Leonie Bennett.
        p. cm. — (I love reading)
    Includes index.
    ISBN-13: 978-1-59716-151-0 (library binding)
    ISBN-10: 1-59716-151-9 (library binding)
    1. Dinosaurs — Juvenile literature. 2. Carnivora, Fossil — Juvenile literature.
    3. Predatory animals — Juvenile literature. I. Title. II. Series.

QE861.5.B452 2005
567.9 — dc22

                          2005029870

For more information, write to Bearport Publishing Company, Inc., 101 Fifth Avenue, Suite 6R, New York, New York 10003. Printed in the United States of America.

10 9 8 7 6 5 4 3 2

The I Love Reading series was originally developed by Tick Tock Media.

CONTENTS

What did dinosaur hunters eat?

Some dinosaurs hunted and ate animals.

These dinosaur hunters
are called **carnivores**.

They all ate meat.

Tyrannosaurus rex
(ti-ran-uh-SOR-uhss REKS)

4

Some dinosaurs ate other dinosaurs.

Some dinosaurs ate other animals.

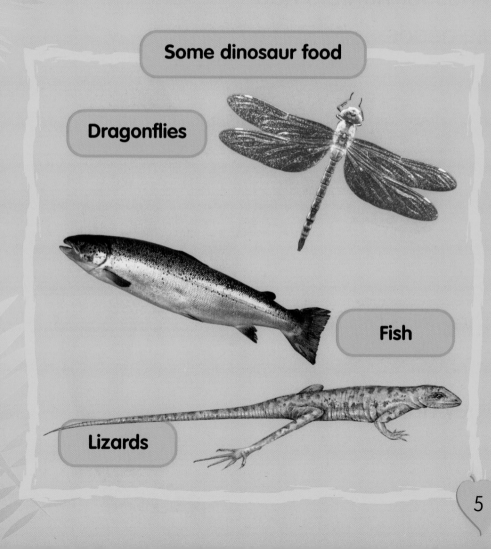

Some dinosaur food

Dragonflies

Fish

Lizards

What did they look like?

Dinosaur hunters had big heads.

They had big teeth.

They had little arms.

Gigantosaurus
(jye-gan-tuh-SOR-uhss)

They had long tails.

They had long
back legs.

7

How big were they?

Some dinosaur hunters were small.

**Compsognathus
(komp-sog-NAY-thuhs)**

Compsognathus was
as small as a cat.

Dinosaur Size

Some dinosaur hunters were big.

Allosaurus
(al-uh-SOR-uhss)

Allosaurus was
as big as a bus.

Dinosaur Size

9

How did they hunt?

Some dinosaurs hunted alone.

Some dinosaurs hunted in a group.

They used their big teeth.

They used their
big **claws**.

Tyrannosaurus rex

Tyrannosaurus rex ate other dinosaurs.

It had **sharp** teeth.

It had two claws on each hand.

This is a Tyrannosaurus rex **fossil**.

Dinosaur Size

Tyrannosaurus rex means
"tyrant lizard king."

Deinonychus
(dye-NON-ih-kuhs)

Deinonychus ran quickly
after its **prey**.

Deinonychus was
very **fierce**.

It had a big brain.

It had very big claws.

Deinonychus means "terrible claw."

Dinosaur Size

Velociraptor
(vuh-LOSS-uh-RAP-tuhr)

Velociraptor looked like a bird.

It had big eyes.

It had a long tail.

Velociraptor means "fast hunter."

Dinosaur Size

Velociraptor had a very big claw on its back foot.

Segnosaurus
(SEG-noh-SOR-uhss)

Segnosaurus means "slow lizard."

It had long arms.

Dinosaur Size

Segnosaurus had feathers.

It had very long claws.

Coelophysis
(see-loh-FYE-sis)

Coelophysis ate lizards and small dinosaurs.

It had a long neck.

Coelophysis ran fast.

It had long, thin back legs.

Coelophysis had sharp claws.

Dinosaur Size

Glossary

carnivores
(KAR-nuh-*vorz*)
meat-eating animals

claws (KLAWZ) sharp nails
at the end of the fingers
or toes of an animal

fierce (FIHRSS)
angry and
dangerous

22

fossil (FOSS-uhl)
very old bones that
have turned into rock

prey (PRAY) animals
that are hunted and
eaten by another animal

sharp (SHARP)
able to cut

23

Index

Learn More

Davis, Kenneth C. *Don't Know Much About Dinosaurs.* New York: HarperCollins (2004).

Dodson, Peter. *An Alphabet of Dinosaurs.* New York: Scholastic Press (1995).

www.childrensmuseum.org/dinosphere/kids/kids_games_level2.html

www.enchantedlearning.com/subjects/dinosaurs/